CHAPTERS IN HISTORY

Did Pilgrims Really Wear Black and White?
And Other Questions About Colonial Times

by Peter and Connie Roop
Illustrated by Ute Simon

■SCHOLASTIC

For Andy, in whose footsteps we gladly walk!
—C. R. and P. R.

ISBN-13: 978-0-439-02522-5
ISBN-10: 0-439-02522-2

Text copyright © 2007 by Peter and Connie Roop
Illustrations copyright © 2007 by Scholastic Inc.

12 11 10 9 8 7 6 5 4 3 2   7 8 9 10 11 12/0

Printed in the U.S.A.
First printing, October 2007

Contents

CHAPTER 1

Who Were the First Americans?

The first people to live in America were
Native Americans. Thousands of years ago,
Alaska and Asia were joined together by
land. This land is called a land bridge. Native

Americans walked over the bridge from Asia into Alaska over twelve thousand years ago. Today, this land bridge is under the ocean.

Coming to a New Land

When the first Native Americans crossed the land bridge, they did not know they were coming to a new land. They were just following the animals they hunted. As years passed, they continued into many parts of North and South America.

There were plenty of animals to hunt. Mighty mammoths roamed the land. Herds of giant bison grazed on grass. There were bears, deer, elk, reindeer, antelope, beavers, ducks, geese, and other animals to hunt.

The Native Americans used the animals in many ways. They ate the meat. They used the skins to make clothes, blankets, and homes. They used the bones to make tools.

Living in Many Places

As the first Americans spread throughout the continent, they settled in different places.

Some Native Americans made their homes in deserts. Some settled high in the mountains. Some lived where it was cold. Others moved onto grassy plains. Many settled in forests along the eastern seashore.

Colonists Meet Native Americans

When the English colonists came to America, they found many Native Americans living here. These Native Americans lived in or near forests. Their way of life depended on what they found in the thick forests.

FACT

These states have Native American names: Mississippi, Massachusetts, Tennessee, Wisconsin, Ohio, the Dakotas, Illinois, Missouri

They hunted deer and bear for food and skins. They gathered wild nuts, berries, and roots. They fished in rivers, lakes, and oceans. They ate clams, oysters, crabs, lobsters, and mussels that lived along the seashore. Many of these Native Americans also grew crops of beans, corn, and squash.

Native American Homes

The Native Americans living in the northern forests built wigwams and longhouses. They made these out of trees and bark. One family lived in a wigwam. Many families shared a longhouse. These homes were warm in the winter.

Many Native Americans lived in the warmer southern forests. They built their homes out of mats. They wove the mats from grass and reeds. These homes let cool breezes in on hot summer days. These Native Americans often lived together in large villages with many homes.

Columbus Comes to America

Millions of Native Americans lived in America when Columbus arrived in 1492. They spoke many different languages. After Columbus came, people from other lands settled in America. But they weren't the first Americans. Native Americans have been living here for thousands of years.

FACT

Columbus thought he had landed on islands called the Indies, so he called the Native Americans that he met *Indians*.

CHAPTER 2

Was Pocahontas Really a Princess?

You've probably heard of Pocahontas. She was the young Native American girl who became friends with an Englishman. But was Pocahontas really a princess?

Chief's Daughter

Pocahontas was born around 1595. She lived in a part of North America that would later become Virginia. Her father, Chief Powhatan, was a very powerful Native American chief. Native Americans did not have kings and queens like the English did.

But Powhatan ruled like a king. Chief Powhatan's people did what he told them to do.

Playful Pocahontas

Powhatan treated Pocahontas like a princess. She did not have to cook, sew, or plant corn like other Native American girls did. She was invited to special dances and feasts.

Pocahontas loved to play. She ran races, danced, sang, played games, and listened to stories. She liked to learn new things.

Meeting John Smith

One day in 1607, Pocahontas's world changed. Three English ships sailed up the James River near where she lived in Virginia. The men aboard the ships had come to build a colony. Captain John Smith was one of their leaders.

Pocahontas was curious about the Englishmen. John Smith visited her village.

He hoped to trade things like bells, beads, cooking pots, and knives with Chief Powhatan. Pocahontas saw that John Smith was brave. And he was kind to Pocahontas.

Becoming Good Friends

John Smith went home to Jamestown. Pocahontas came to visit him. She taught him words in her language. He taught Pocahontas words in English. They became good friends.

GAME

Can you match the Native American words to the English words?

1. shoe
2. bed
3. friend
4. fire
5. dog

a. mawchick
b. moccasin
c. pokatawer
d. attemous
e. tuffan

1b, 2e, 3a, 4c, 5d

Pocahontas was sad when John Smith sailed back to England. She thought she would never see him again.

Visiting England

Years later, Pocahontas married an Englishman named John Rolfe. She spoke English. She wore English clothes. She sailed with John Rolfe to England.

Pocahontas was treated like a princess in two countries! She went to dances. She went to feasts. She even met the king and queen of England! John Smith came to see her.

Pocahontas missed her home in Virginia. But before she could leave England, she got sick and died. Pocahontas was only twenty-two years old.

Today there is a statue of Pocahontas in England.

CHAPTER 3

Who Helped the Pilgrims to Survive?

A Native American named Squanto helped the Pilgrims in two important ways. He taught the Pilgrims how to live in the American wilderness. And he helped the Pilgrims communicate with the Native Americans.

The Pilgrims were very surprised when they met Squanto in the spring of 1621. The Pilgrims were excited because Squanto spoke English. He had lived in Europe and learned English there.

Squanto Helps the Pilgrims

Squanto lived with the Pilgrims for many months. During that time, Squanto showed the Pilgrims how much he could help them.

First he helped them find food. The Pilgrims had lived in cities in England. They were not farmers and hunters. When the Pilgrims came to America they did not know what wild plants they could eat. They did not know the best places to hunt deer, ducks, geese, and turkeys. They did not know where to catch fish. They did not know how to plant corn, beans, or squash so they would grow well.

Plymouth, Massachusetts

Squanto had lived in the area we now call Massachusetts. His people had hunted, fished, and grown crops there. The Pilgrims planted their first crops in the same fields where Squanto's family had once farmed. When he was a boy, Squanto had learned how to plant corn so it grew well. He taught the Pilgrims how his Wampanoag people planted corn.

Growing Corn

Squanto told the Pilgrims he needed fish to make the corn grow better. The Pilgrims were puzzled. *"How could fish make corn grow better?"* they wondered. Squanto showed them.

Squanto was a member of the Patuxet tribe which was part of the Wampanogs.

Squanto dug a hole. He put three fish in the bottom of the hole. Then he dropped in the seeds of corn. He covered the corn and fish with dirt.

The Pilgrims asked Squanto why he put the fish in the hole with the seeds. He said that when the fish began to rot, it would make food for the corn. This food would help the corn grow taller and stronger.

Squanto showed the Pilgrims the best places to hunt and fish. He showed them which plants they could eat.

Native Americans Become Friends

Squanto could speak English and the Algonquin language so he helped the Pilgrims communicate with the Native Americans.

The Pilgrims wanted to be friendly with the Native Americans. With Squanto's help, the Native Americans and Pilgrims agreed to get along. These peaceful times lasted for fifty years.

Squanto helped the Pilgrims to survive by showing them how to grow corn and find food. Squanto also helped the Pilgrims and Native Americans live together peacefully. The Pilgrims had much to thank Squanto for.

CHAPTER 4

What Did the Pilgrims Really Eat at the First Thanksgiving?

Can you imagine eating eel at Thanksgiving dinner? The Pilgrims did!

Do you have pumpkin pie for Thanksgiving dessert? The Pilgrims had pumpkins, but no pie. Why? They had no wheat to make pie crust.

Do you eat turkey for Thanksgiving? The Pilgrims probably did. But we do not know for sure. We do know that the Pilgrims ate geese, ducks, lobsters, clams, deer, fish, crabs, oysters, and eels at their Thanksgiving feast.

Do you have cranberries on Thanksgiving? The Pilgrims did. They also ate blackberries, blueberries, and wild grapes.

Do you enjoy potatoes on Thanksgiving? The Pilgrims did not. They didn't have potatoes. But they did have beans, squash, and corn.

Native Americans Join the Pilgrims

Do you have company for Thanksgiving? The Pilgrims sure did! Over ninety Native Americans joined the Pilgrims for their first Thanksgiving.

Harvest Celebrations

Native Americans had their own harvest celebration before winter began. Each season they celebrated and gave thanks for the food they hunted, grew, and gathered.

A time of giving thanks was not new to the Pilgrims, either. When they lived in England, the Pilgrims had celebrated the Harvest

Festival. This fall festival was held when the crops were harvested. After their first year in America, the Pilgrims wanted to give thanks for their own harvest. They decided to have a Thanksgiving celebration. And their new Native American friends joined them.

Hunting and Gathering Food

So how did the Pilgrims get their food? They could not go to a store. There were no stores in Plymouth in 1621.

The Pilgrims grew corn, beans, pumpkins, and squash. They hunted deer, geese, ducks, and turkeys. They gathered clams, oysters, crabs, and lobsters from the ocean. They fished in rivers and streams. And they caught wiggly, squiggly eels with their hands. They found nuts in the forest. They picked cranberries, blueberries, and blackberries.

Three-day Celebration

The first Thanksgiving lasted for three days! The Pilgrims and the Native Americans ate many meals together over the long celebration. The Native Americans brought five deer to the feast. They wanted to make sure there was enough food for everyone.

The Pilgrims and Native Americans played games. They ran races against each other. The Pilgrims marched. The Native Americans danced special dances. The Pilgrims demonstrated how to use their guns. The Native Americans shot arrows at targets.

Each night everyone slept well. They were tired from all the cooking, eating, and celebrating.

Getting Ready for Winter

When the Thanksgiving celebration ended, the Native Americans returned to their homes. They had many things to do to get ready for winter. The Pilgrims also started to get ready for the cold winter ahead.

We remember the Pilgrims and Native Americans today by giving thanks and enjoying many of the same foods they shared at the First Thanksgiving.

Stewed Pumpkin

4 c. cooked squash or pumpkin, mashed
3 Tbl. butter
2 tsp. cider vinegar
1 tsp. ground ginger
½ tsp. salt

Put all of the ingredients in a saucepan. Stir over medium heat on the stove. Serve hot. Mmmm!

CHAPTER 5

Did Pilgrims Really Wear Black and White?

When you see a picture of Pilgrims, they are wearing black-and-white clothes. They have tall black hats. They have silver buckles on their black shoes.

Guess what? The Pilgrims did wear black-and-white clothes, but they also wore red, green, blue, purple, brown, and gray clothes! And they did not have buckles on their hats or shoes.

Explaining the Mix-up

Why do we think the Pilgrims only wore black-and-white clothes? One story says the mix-up comes from the word "sad." One Pilgrim wrote in a journal that his leader wore "sad" clothes. To modern readers, it sounds like his clothes were black. But "sad" did not mean unhappy to the Pilgrims. "Sad" meant dark. A "sad" green coat was a dark green coat!

Two Sets of Clothes

Most Pilgrims had two sets of clothes. They wore their best clothes on Sundays when they went to church. These clothes may have been black and white. During the rest of the week, the Pilgrims wore their colorful work clothes.

Dressing in Many Layers

Pilgrim girls dressed just like their mothers. Boys dressed just like their fathers. When they were very young, Pilgrim girls and boys both wore dresses! These dresses were easy to put on, take off, and clean.

Older girls wore many layers of clothes. Getting dressed in the morning took a long time. First, girls put on a petticoat. Next, they pulled on long, red wool stockings. Two more petticoats were added. The third petticoat was like a long skirt. Girls tied on an apron. Then, they put on a jacket with buttons. Girls wore small white caps indoors and outdoors. Finally, girls put on leather shoes.

Wearing Work Clothes

Boys did not wear as many clothes as girls. Boys wore long stockings and leather shoes.

They wore shirts.
Their jackets had no
sleeves. This was so
their arms were free
for chopping wood,
fishing, hunting, and
taking care of farm
animals. Boys' pants
came to just below
their knees. Boys
wore caps or hats
only when outside.
They wore shoes in
the winter and went
barefoot in the summer.

One last step in
getting dressed for boys
and girls—they tied on
their pockets! That's
right. Pilgrim clothes

FACT

The Pilgrims
did not have
left shoes or
right shoes.
Both shoes
were exactly
the same!

did not have pockets. A pocket was a small leather bag. Both girls and boys wore pockets in which they carried things they needed.

Colorful Clothes

Pilgrim's clothes were very colorful. Their stockings might have been red, green, or brown. Skirts and pants might have been brown, gray, or green. Jackets might have been red, green, blue, or black. Caps and hats were red, brown, and green.

Did the Pilgrims were black and white? They sure did, but they wore many other colors, too!

CHAPTER 6

Did Colonial Children Go to School?

The first colonial children did not have to go to school. Why not? There were no schools in early colonial times! The first school opened in Boston in 1635. Later, as more children were born, more schools began.

Working at Home

Life was very busy for the first colonists. They had to build homes. They had to plant crops. They had to care for their farm animals.

Colonial girls and boys helped their parents. Boys carried water and firewood. They fed the chickens, goats, cows, horses, and sheep. They went hunting and helped with the crops. Girls sewed clothes. They cooked. They took care of their little brothers and sisters. They helped in the gardens.

But parents wanted their children to learn how to read, write, and do arithmetic. However, there wasn't much time for lessons.

Dame Schools

Dame schools were the first schools. A dame school was held in someone's home. A "dame", or woman, had children come to her home and classes were held there. She taught them their ABC's, a little arithmetic, and a few Bible verses. Usually the dame did her own housework while the children studied their lessons. Dame schools were like today's kindergarten classes.

Town Schools

As colonial towns began to grow, there were enough children for real schools.

Families that lived in towns built the first schools. Teachers were hired. These schools had one room and many were just for boys. Boys who lived on farms walked into town to go to school.

Sometimes girls were allowed to go to school with the boys. But then the girls sat on one side of the room. The boys sat on the other.

Colonial Teachers

Most colonial teachers were men. They were called schoolmasters.

Schoolmasters were rarely paid with money. They were paid with corn, firewood, or food.

FACT

Lessons were
called the 3 R's:
1. Reading
2. 'Riting
3. 'Rithmetic

Many schoolmasters did not have their own homes. They lived with their students! A schoolmaster would live with one family for two weeks. Then he would move in with another family. Imagine if your teacher came home with you at night!

Reading

There were not many books in the colonies. Books cost a lot of money. Most families had just one book, the Bible.

Many colonial children learned to read with a horn book. A horn book was made out of wood. A piece of paper with the ABC's and words was put onto the wood. The paper was covered with a thin piece of horn from a cow. The cow horn protected the paper from

tearing. The letters and words could be read through the thin horn.

'Riting

Students did not write on paper. Instead, they wrote on a flat rock called slate. They wrote their letters and numbers on the slate with chalk.

Later, when there was more paper, students wrote with quill pens. A quill pen is made from a goose or turkey feather.

Students dipped their feathers into a pot of ink. The students could only write two or three letters at a time. Then they had to dip the pen back into the ink. They also had to be very, very careful not to drip ink on their paper! Learning to write took a long time.

'Rithmetic

Colonial children also learned arithmetic. They learned how to add, subtract, multiply, and divide. Students needed these skills for different jobs when they grew up.

Best "R" of All

Colonial children had a fourth "R" they enjoyed the most, recess! At recess they wrestled, ran races, and played games. The teacher rang a bell by hand to end recess. Is recess your favorite "R," too?

CHAPTER 7

What Games Did Colonial Children Play?

Colonial children had to spend a lot of time helping their parents and going to school. But, just like you, they always found time to play. What kinds of games did they play? Let's find out!

Large Families

Most colonial families had many children so there was always a brother or sister to play with. Sometimes relatives or friends from faraway came for a long visit. And as more people settled in towns, there were even more children to play with.

Mixing Fun with Work

Colonial children had many chores to do every day. Often colonial children found a way to play while they worked. Boys and girls gathering eggs might have made a contest to see who could fill an egg basket first. They made a game of chasing runaway pigs back into their pens. Singing or whistling while they worked helped many colonial children enjoy doing their jobs.

Making Their Own Toys

Colonial children made many of their own toys. Boys made marbles out of clay. They dried the round clay balls in the sun to make them hard. Girls made dolls out of rags or corn cobs. They dressed them in clothes they sewed from scraps of cloth. Girls and boys liked to roll round hoops. The hoops came from old barrels. Sometimes, they raced the hoops by pushing them with a stick. Jackstraws were like pick-up sticks. They were made from hay or long wood splinters. Each straw had to be picked from a pile without moving any of the others.

> **FACT**
>
> Sometimes boys used round pebbles as marbles.

Playing Outside

Tag, running races, leapfrog, tug-of-war, and wrestling were popular outside games. Many children liked to play Blindman's Buff. One child was blindfolded and had to find the other children playing the game. Many

towns had special grassy places for bowling.
Swimming in a pond or creek on hot summer
days was fun, too. Cold winter days meant it
was time for skating, sledding, and throwing
snowballs.

Work Hard, Play Hard

At the end of the day colonial children were tired from helping their families. But they always found time to have fun. In the evenings, they relaxed by telling riddles and practicing tongue twisters. Here's one for you to try: "Six shy shavers sheared six shy sheep."

FACT

Colonial girls called their dolls "poppets."

RIDDLES

1. What falls down, but never gets hurt?
2. Which side of an apple is the reddest?

1. Rain; 2. The out-SIDE

CHAPTER 8

How Did the Thirteen Colonies Get Their Names?

New Hampshire

Massachusetts (Maine)

New York

Rhode Island

Connecticut

Pennsylvania

New Jersey

Virginia

Delaware

Maryland

North Carolina

South Carolina

Georgia

Atlantic Ocean

After the English settled in Virginia and Massachusetts, more people wanted to come to America. They wanted to make new colonies.

A colony is a new land where people from another country come to live. Before long, thirteen colonies stretched from Canada in the north to Florida in the south.

Thirteen Colonies

People from England and other countries came to America to build farms and towns. Many also wanted religious freedom.

The colonists sent wood, fish, and crops back to England. Many colonists also traded with Native Americans for furs. The thick beaver, fox, mink, and otter furs were made into hats, coats, and capes in England and other countries.

FACT

A colony is still ruled by another country's laws and leaders.

By 1732 there were thirteen English colonies. The colonies can be divided into three groups: New England, the Middle Colonies, and the Southern Colonies.

Four New England Colonies

The Pilgrims landed in Massachusetts in 1620. Massachusetts was named after the Native American people called the Massachusetts. They lived in the area before

the Pilgrims came.

Connecticut became a colony in 1662. The Connecticut settlers named their colony after the Connecticut River.

Rhode Island was the smallest colony. Rhode Island became a colony in 1663. The Dutch, who first came to this area, named the colony Rhode Island because an island off the coast resembled the Greek island of Rhodes.

New Hampshire became a colony in 1679. New Hampshire was named after Hampshire in England. The colonists of New Hampshire were famous for the tall trees they cut down.

41

Four Colonies in the Middle

The Dutch had a colony along the Hudson River. They called it New Amsterdam. In 1664 the English captured New Amsterdam. They called their colony New York to honor the king's brother James who was the Duke of York.

For a while New Jersey was part of New York. New Jersey became a separate colony in 1664. It was named after "Jersey," an English island.

Pennsylvania became a colony in 1681. It was founded by William Penn. Pennsylvania means Penn's Woods. *Sylvania* means woods in Latin.

Delaware was named after Baron De La Warr from Virginia. Delaware had been part of New York and Pennsylvania. In 1704 Delaware became a separate colony.

Five Southern Colonies

Virginia was the first English colony in America. In 1607 the English began their colony at Jamestown.

Virginia was named for Queen Elizabeth I who never married.

Maryland is Delaware's neighbor. It became a colony in 1634. Maryland was named "Mary's Land" after Queen Henrietta Maria, the wife of King Charles I.

The Carolina colony was started in 1663. The word Carolina comes from *Carolus*, the Latin name of King Charles I. In 1729, the

Carolina colony was split into two colonies, North Carolina and South Carolina.

Georgia became a colony in 1732. Georgia was named after King George II. Georgia was the most southern English colony. Its neighbor was Florida, a colony of Spain.

The United States Is Born!

These first thirteen colonies are very important to the history of America. They became the first thirteen states when the Declaration of Independence was signed on July 4, 1776. How many states are there now?